Envision Your Best Life and Live It

For Middle School Students:

8 Mistakes for 6th, 7th and 8th Grade Students to
Avoid When Materializing
& 8 Be-Do-Have Steps to Overcome Challenges
that Will Unleash the Power of Your Imagination

Alexandria Patterson

Published by Mastercraft Avenue Publishing
Astronomically Prosperous LLC

DISCLAIMER

The advice contained in this material might not be suitable for everyone. The author designed the information to present her opinion about the subject matter. The reader must carefully investigate all aspects of any decision before committing himself or herself. The author obtained the information contained herein from sources she believes to be reliable and from her own personal experience, but she neither implies nor intends any guarantee of accuracy. The author nor the publishers claim to be doctors. Please consult professionals for any mental, physical and emotional assistance. The author particularly disclaims any liability, loss, or risk taken by individuals who directly or indirectly act on the information contained herein. The author believes the advice presented here is sound, but readers cannot hold her responsible for either the actions they take or the risk taken by individuals who directly or indirectly act on the information contained herein.

Other Books from Author:

*Envision Your Best Life and Live It:
12 Mistakes for Young Adults to Avoid
When Manifesting & 12 Be-Do-Have Steps
To Overcome Challenges That Will
Unleash The Power Of Your Imagination*

DEDICATION

For my current and future sons and daughters

QUOTES

"Imagining Creates Reality"
-Neville Goddard

"Imagination is more important than knowledge."
-Albert Einstein

"It's time to start living the life you've imagined."
-Henry James

"By faith, we understand that the worlds were framed by the word of God so that the things which are seen were not made of things which are visible."

-Hebrews 11:3 (New King James Version)

TABLE OF CONTENTS

INTRODUCTION

A Brief Story of My Early Beginnings into Manifesting

Growing up, I often found myself alone, left behind while my younger brother and cousins went away for summers with their father's side of the family. I was the oldest grandchild of five, and an overprotected child, but my solitude became a canvas for creativity. I spent hours singing and dancing in front of the mirror, writing imaginary stories, and imitating characters from movies I watched over and over again. I learned early on that my imagination was a powerful tool, one that helped me create my own world when I felt isolated from the one around me.

When I was in middle school, I lived in a neighborhood that had gang violence in Watts, California, for three years with my aunt and cousins. While living in Watts, I was scared, but I found comfort and inspiration in the music of Lauryn Hill. One line from her song "Miseducation of Lauryn Hill" stuck with me: "I looked at my environment and wondered where the fire went, what happened to everything we used to be." That word, "environment," stayed with me. Even as a young girl, I realized I didn't have to accept my surroundings as

1

they were. I could use my imagination to picture something different, something better.

I started to imagine a different environment for myself and my family—a calmer, safer place to live. At the time, I didn't have the words to articulate what I was doing, but I was intentionally using my imagination to create a vision of a better reality. A year later, we moved to a quiet street on the other side of town, off Slauson and Crenshaw. For two years, I lived there with my aunt and cousins, and the calm I had imagined became our daily experience. Even when I moved back to Watts to live with my mother, the neighborhood had become calmer, almost as if my vision had helped materialize a change.

From that point on, I began to see my imagination not as an escape, but as a powerful tool—a tool that could shape my experiences and bring about real change. I learned to intentionally use my imagination to create better scenarios, not just for myself, but for those around me.

Why This Book

I gathered my experiences together in this book to show that you have this same power. Your imagination is not just a place to retreat to; it's a source of strength and creativity that can help you overcome challenges and materialize (make material or matter) the desires of your heart. I want to share my journey with you and show you how you can use your imagination to create the life you truly want to live. This book is a guide to help you unlock that potential (power), to help you envision (make, put in + thing seen) your best life and make it your reality.

This book will help students who have challenges academically or focusing on no stimulating tasks. The experiences I share in this book have nothing to do with traditional academics and everything to do with day to day life within our own individual world (literally means "human existence").

You, The Reader

By reading this book, you acknowledge your role as the CREATOR OF YOUR OWN REALITY. This book serves as a gentle reminder of the steps you are already taking and provides new tools, techniques, and strategies to further aid you to materialize the life you envision (to make or put into sight or imagination). You hold the power to design your existence on all levels - physical, mental, emotional, and spiritual. Embrace your vision for yourself, your household, your community, and even the planet. This book aims to clarify the intentional materialization process you are already doing every day. Understand that with an open mind, you can be more intentional and persistent in creating your desired reality. As you absorb the information, keep in mind that you are already familiar with some of these tools and techniques; now is the time to put them into action. Embrace the knowledge that you are the creator of your reality and anticipate the joy of applying these teachings in your life.

Who Am I?

Hi, I'm Alexandria, and my mission is to help people bring their inner visions to reality. Sometimes, figuring out how to make your vision a reality is tough, but I'm here to guide you every step of the way. Throughout the book, I share with you my experiences of creating my own reality through my imagination and other techniques. Have you ever had a tough time getting what you wanted (desired)? I've been there. I understand what it's like to feel stuck and not knowing how to get what I want especially in middle school. It can be frustrating, and sometimes it feels like you're just going through the motions. But everything changed when I took the time to learn from others who were excelling.

I started to look into their journeys and discovered that many successful people have a formula that they follow. They also use their stories to inspire others, which I aim to do as well. I've made mistakes and learned valuable lessons along the way. It wasn't until I looked to those who had achieved true success that I began to see the steps I needed to follow. I've gathered all these insights into a book designed to help you bring your own vision to life.

The key to this journey lies in recognizing your potential (power) and being creative in approaching your goals. It all starts with having a vision and understanding your own unique story. There's so much power in using your own story to shape your vision, and I'm excited to help you begin this incredible journey.

The 3 Parts: BE, DO, HAVE

This book is designed around three parts: BE, DO, and HAVE. Each part focuses on specific chapters that guide you through what you need to *be*, *do*, and *have* in the process of materializing your wants.

In the **BE** section, you'll find chapters on Vision and Desire. From my personal experience, materialization begins with taking in the very things you want to see in your life. I've learned that to achieve (perform or accomplish) your vision and fulfill your wants or desires, you first need to *become* them. When I visualized my goals and felt the reality of them in my mind, I naturally began to attract what I longed for.

The **DO** section contains chapters on Imagination, the Power of Thoughts & Words, the Subconscious (under or below + knowing or aware), and Copying someone. Bringing what you imagine into matter or material isn't just about wishing—it's about *doing* the work, which I like to call the "fun"! The actions in this section are key to bringing your vision to life. Whether it's using your imagination or tapping into the power of your thoughts and words, the *doing* part is where things start to move.

Finally, in the **HAVE** section, you'll dive into chapters on your W.H.Y., and practice Gratitude & Appreciation. Without this critical piece, it's easy to get sidetracked, distracted, or frustrated. This section is all about maintaining focus and commitment so that you can *have* what you've materialized with clarity and joy.

Your "Mistakes to Avoid"

In each chapter, I share the mistakes I've personally made while pursuing my desires, and I'm committed to helping you avoid making those same mistakes. Materialization is a powerful process, but it's easy to get off track if you're not focused. My goal is to offer you insight into the lessons I've learned so that you can navigate your own journey with greater ease and clarity.

For each mistake, I offer a practical solution you can apply in the "Next Step" sections to avoid falling into the same traps. This approach is designed to keep you focused on your vision and desires, helping you stay aligned with your goals while minimizing setbacks. By being aware of these possible mistakes early on, you'll be better prepared to move forward with clarity and confidence, making your path to materialization more direct and fulfilling.

Your "Next Step"

At the end of each chapter, you'll find a section called "Next Step," which is specifically designed to help you put the ideas and concepts into action. This isn't just about reading or understanding the material—it's about *doing* something with it. Each "Next Step" offers a practical exercise, reflection, or action item that will encourage you to take what you've learned and apply it in a real and tangible way to your life.

As you move through the book, taking these steps is how you'll begin to actively shape your reality. These exercises are more than just tasks; they are small, deliberate actions that help you align with your vision and desires. By consistently engaging with them after each chapter, you'll be making steady progress toward realizing your dreams. This approach ensures that you're not just absorbing information but taking meaningful strides toward your goals, empowering you to materialize your desires with intention and purpose.

Throughout this book, there are words I will provide meanings using ETYMOLOGY (to study the true sense and original meaning of a word) in parenthesis "( )". You may have recognized this already in previous paragraphs. The only time you WILL NOT see original meanings in "( )" is when I am breaking down the meaning usually in the first or second paragraph of a section.

I am using etymonline.com to define words.

Part 1 - BE

You already have the vision and desire within you, and now it's time to bring them to life. The word 'Be' can be broken down to "I Am" or "Exist," and in Latin, it is the perfect past tense "I Was." So, to 'Be' your vision and desire, you already 'ARE' your vision and desire.

1

Vision

What is Vision?

Before we get started on your vision of your life or this academic school year, let's break down the word "vision." In etymology, vision means 'something seen in the imagination.' In Latin, the word 'vision' comes from *visionem,* which is "act of seeing, sight, thing seen."

What do you see for yourself?

Living your life is about envisioning what you care to do, become, and have. What is your vision? Envision your future for yourself, your family, your community, your loved ones, and maybe even the planet. Your vision should be impactful. When we admire the lives of others, we often forget that where they are now may result from their own aspirations (action of breathing into) and hard work. We overlook their struggles and the journey they had to undertake to achieve their goals. Everyone has a story, even those who are now wealthy and successful. Many of them came from humble beginnings, facing poverty and hardship. They had to use their imagination and determination to overcome their circumstances.

Vision is the starting point of all achievement. It is the map that guides you through the complex, winding paths of life. Without a vision, you might find yourself stuck or going in circles, unsure of your purpose or destination. But with a clear vision, you can navigate through the darkest of times, making decisions that align with your deepest desires and values. Think of vision as your inner compass, pointing you in the direction that aligns with your true self. It is more than just a fleeting dream or a vague wish; it is a powerful force that, when nurtured, becomes the foundation upon which you build your life.

Vision vs. Reality: The Bridge of Action

While vision is where it all begins, it is not where it ends. A vision without action is like a seed without soil—it holds potential, but it will never grow unless it is planted, nurtured, and given the right conditions to flourish. This is where your imagination comes into play. Imagination is the bridge between vision and reality. It is the tool that allows you to see beyond your current circumstances and visualize a future where your dreams have come to life. But vision and imagination alone are not enough. They must be accompanied by dedication (the giving of oneself to some purpose), resilience (act of rebounding or springing back), and a willingness to take action.

Think of all the people who have made a significant impact on the planet. From the great leaders who fought for freedom to the scientists who dared to challenge conventional thinking, to the artists who inspired generations with their creativity—what did they all have in common? They had a vision, and they were willing to do whatever it took to bring that vision to life. They didn't just imagine a better future; they believed in it so deeply that they were compelled to act on it. They faced countless obstacles, failures, and setbacks, but their vision kept them moving forward.

Crafting Your Vision: The Power of Clarity

Let's focus on your academic school. To create a vision for your academic school year, start by getting clear on what truly matters to you. Ask yourself: What do I want my first semester, second semester or next school year to look like? What kind of person do I want to be? What impact do I want to have on the people around me? Think beyond material success. Consider what means a lot to you, what you enjoy doing, and what you see yourself doing.

Visualize it in vivid (animated, lively) detail. Don't just think about what you want; see it in your imagination. Picture the colors, the sounds, the feelings associated with your vision. Allow yourself to dream big without limitations or fear. When you are clear about your vision, it will serve as a source of motivation (stem from the word "motive" which means moving, motion), guiding your choices and actions. Every decision you make, big or small, will be influenced by your vision. When faced with challenges, you will find the strength to persevere (from "per" meaning 'very' + "severus" meaning 'strict') because you know where you're headed.

My Lack of Vision with Getting into My Middle School's Band

I grew up loving the sound of drums, though I never told anyone I wanted to play music. One day in 6th grade, I attended a school assembly and was shocked to see my cousin—who was the same age as me—performing in our middle school band. I had no idea he played music. As I watched him on trumpet, my eyes drifted past him and landed on the snare drum and bass drum. At that moment, I knew I wanted to play one of those instruments.

Since my cousin and I lived together, I asked him questions about the band. My biggest question was, *"How can I get in?"* He told me, *"You have to be in the magnet program."* But I wasn't in the magnet program.

Determined, I asked my aunt to take me to the school so we could find out how I might join. She spoke with the magnet program coordinator, who pulled up my test scores. The coordinator explained that my scores weren't high enough for the program. I was crushed. After that meeting, I gave up and never tried to join the band for the rest of middle school years.

Looking back, I realize something important. Before that meeting, I never closed my eyes to *see* myself in the band. I never wrote down a vision or imagined myself playing drums no matter what obstacles came my way. Without that vision, I allowed the coordinator's words to stop me from chasing something I had wanted since I was five years old—playing the drums.

Mistake to Avoid: Going After What You Want Without A Vision

A person who lacks vision is like a wanderer, moving aimlessly without direction or purpose. Without a clear idea of where you're headed, every step or choice feels uncertain. Life becomes a series of reactions instead of intentional decisions, leading to confusion, frustration, and a sense of drifting without purpose.

Had I taken time to visualize myself playing drums, I possibly would have had another plan to still play drums outside of my middle school. Had I taken the time to write my vision down and got clear on what I wanted to do with playing drums in other places outside middle school, that magnet coordinator's "No" to me joining magnet to get in band, I would have found other ways to play drums.

Without a vision, you allow life to happen to you instead of actively shaping it. You end up living out someone else's plans or expectations, missing out on opportunities that align with your true desires and purpose. The danger of having no vision is that it leads to stagnation—you may be busy, but you're not moving forward toward something meaningful.

Having a clear vision is like possessing a compass. It doesn't just tell you what direction to go; it helps you make informed decisions along the way. It acts as a filter, allowing you to discern which paths are worth pursuing and which are distractions. It motivates you to get up each morning with a sense of purpose and determination, guiding your steps with intention.

When you avoid the mistake of living without vision, you empower yourself to lead a life of clarity and fulfillment. You no longer accept whatever comes your way; instead, you deliberately create the future you want. Vision is what turns dreams into actionable goals, and it's the driving force that allows you to overcome obstacles and setbacks with resilience.

Taking the First Step

Exercise: Write down or draw your vision map that you would like to see happen in your life. If drawing a vision map for your "life" is too much, draw one for your academic school year.

Journal prompt: "What's one or two opportunities I want to envision for this school year, even if it feels impossible right now?"

Now, do not worry about having the perfect responses or that your responses might change in the future. The exercise and journal prompt is to help you see what is possible!

2

Desire

To have what you desire, you must have a burning desire. When we break down the word "desire," it originates from the Latin word "desideri," which means to wish, long for, expect, or demand. The word "desider" is derived from 'the stars', and "sider" or "sidious" or "siderious" refers to 'heavenly bodies and star constellations'.

What is it you long for? What are your expectations for your future? What do you aspire to be, do, or have?

Having delved into the etymology of the word "desire," we now possess a deeper understanding of what we truly long for. This heightened awareness guides our thoughts on the expectations we hold for the lives we are creating for ourselves.

The word "desire" is synonymous with "goal," which means 'purpose' or 'something one hopes or intends to accomplish' according to the Merriam-Webster dictionary.

Let's also discuss the word "want". Many times we use the word "want" when we refer to something. The word "want" has a few meanings, but let's focus on two of the meanings in particular. "Want" means 'lack (absence, shortage)', but "want" also means "desire". If you reread the etymology of "desire" at the beginning of this chapter, you will see that the word "want" is NOT in "desire" etymology or meaning. This means that the word "desire" is a higher level of "want".

One way to figure out your desires is to have a conversation with yourself. Look at what is possibly missing in your life and consider the people you admire and the things you aspire to. When going after what you desire, here are some questions to consider:

- Will what I desire bring me joy?
- Will this make me a better person?
- Will this help me grow?
- Can this make me money?
- Is this solving a problem for others?

If you see yourself getting excited or finding something missing, consider going for it.

Clarity! Be Clear about Your Desires

Once you have clarified your desires and answered the initial questions, take some time to write them down. Delve into detail, getting specific about what you want to have, do, or be. For the person you aspire to be, jot down possible characteristics, such as daily wardrobe, social circle, and friendships desires. If it's material possessions you want, visualize and detail them. Consider how they will enhance your life and make you a better person and even how these things will help others around you. Think about the actions that will lead to your desires, considering the importance and worth of investing time and money into them. Keep the initial questions and statements in mind as you proceed.

Jot down your desires on sticky notes, small pieces of paper, or laminated index cards and place them in the places you frequent, whether at home on your bedroom wall, in your notebooks for school or even your cellphone. Having these reminders in the places you frequent can remind yourself what you are working towards and what you hope to achieve. These reminders constantly reinforce your goals or desires, helping you stay focused and committed. By reading them frequently, you will continually be reminded of your mission for the day and the steps you need to take to move closer to your goal. This will provide the guidance and motivation to work towards your aspirations.

The most significant step in achieving your desires is to believe they are attainable. Identify your desires and embrace them as part of your vision.

Research, Re-Search, RESEARCH!

Now, let's discuss researching your desire. Whether it's something you desire to be, have, or do, it's essential to learn some things about your desire. Understanding the background, origins, and purpose of your desire will give you a deeper connection and a better understanding of its significance. Consider taking personal photos or visiting the place you desire, if you can. For example, if you are looking to get on a sports team at your school or learn to play an instrument, find out what the requirements are for you to participate. If it's a person or a profession you aspire to, engage in meaningful conversations with individuals already in that profession. Ask questions about what they enjoy about it and what led them to pursue it. The more you delve into your desires and understand them, the more they resonate with you. This deeper understanding will guide you in determining whether these desires truly align with your soul. Make certain to have your parents or guardian assist you in your research or guide you through it.

My Story of How Desire with Clarity and Research Result Accomplishment

One key to staying committed is understanding exactly what your goal or desire really involves. I faced this lesson when I tried to get into my middle school band. I didn't do any research before asking my aunt to take me to the school and see if I could join the magnet program.

Ironically, I became clear on *why* I wanted to be in the band only after the coordinator told me "no." My biggest reasons were wanting to get out of the house, learn how to read music, and, of course, play it.

Before seeing my cousin perform in the middle school band and trying to join myself, I had already discovered an interest in guitar. The summer before middle school, I spent a weekend at my father's house where my older stepsister showed me how to play a little.

After being turned down for the magnet program, I shared with my 6th grade teacher that I really wanted to learn guitar. I was eager to be like my favorite musician at the time—Lauryn Hill. My teacher encouraged me: *"Ask your parents to buy you a guitar. The worst they can say is 'no.'"*

I took her advice and asked my mom. That Christmas, my granny bought me a guitar, and the following school year I started personal guitar lessons. My mom and granny even teamed up to cover the cost of lessons for an entire year.

Taking my teacher's advice to simply ask was the best step I could have taken. My mom and granny did the research to find the right guitar and a teacher, and because of that, I got to pursue what I truly desired.

Mistake to Avoid: Lack of Clarity and Research

Not having clarity nor researching will make your goal and vision tough to stay committed to. When you aren't clear about what you truly want or fail to research the necessary steps to achieve it, your desire becomes shaky, and you won't stay committed. Without clarity, you can't visualize the end result, which makes it harder to stay motivated, especially when challenges arise.

I learned this the hard way after as soon as I got the "no" from the magnet program coordinator. After being told "no" to getting in the magnet program for the band, I realized my clear reason for joining the band. Once I let my mother and granny know I was interested in playing guitar, they did the research for me. I stayed committed for a year in personal lessons.

Without clarity, it's easy to get lost in the process. The desire may be there, but the lack of direction causes delays, confusion, and frustration. You find yourself wandering aimlessly, wondering why things aren't falling into place. For me, the turning point was after the magnet coordinator told me "no". I immediately took playing music seriously and got clear on playing music would get me out the house and having an extra curricular activity that brought me joy.

Research is equally important. It's what transforms a vague dream into a concrete, achievable plan. When I told my mother and granny I wanted to play guitar, they got me all I needed to get started by researching for me because I didn't know where to look. At that time, the internet was still fairly new.

The mistake of not having clarity or doing research is common when pursuing a desire. It leaves you open to distractions, delays, and ultimately, disappointment. When you aren't clear, you'll find it harder to persevere because you can't see the finish line. When you don't research, you lack the practical knowledge to make informed decisions, leading to wasted time, energy, and resources.

Avoiding this mistake means taking the time to get clear on your desire. Ask yourself: Will this bring me joy? What am I really doing this for? Once you have that clarity, dive into the research. Find out what steps are required, who can help you, and what potential obstacles might arise. The combination of clarity and research ensures that your desire is not just a fleeting wish but a well-thought-out plan that you can commit to wholeheartedly.

Your Next Step

Exercise: Use the vision list you wrote from chapter 1. Now add a clear reason and what research you and your guardian may have to do.

Journal Prompt: What would having one of these dreams come true mean for me right now?

Again, don't worry about having a perfect answer or that your mind may change later.

PART 2 - DO

Engage in the joy of using your imagination, use your subconscious with intention (comes from word "intend" which means 'direct one's attention to') learn from others, use the power of your thoughts and words with intention. 'DO' means "to perform, execute, achieve, carry out, or bring to pass by the procedure of any kind."

3

Imagination

What is Imagination?

When we look at the definition of 'imagination,' it means "faculty of the mind that manipulates images," when we get down to the etymology of imagination, the stem 'imaginari' means to "form an image." The word "image" in Latin comes from "imaginem" meaning 'copy, imitation, likeness, statue, picture.'

Now is the time to unleash your imagination.

This is your chance to imagine exactly what you want to be, do, and have in this material world (human existence). Start by crafting a narrative. Develop the story of what you desire to do using the questions in the chapter where you identified your desires. Then, gather images from various sources like books, magazines, newspapers, and online articles to create a vision board for yourself. Make it large enough to see daily, whether on a cardboard box or your bedroom wall. Utilize images of other people doing the things you want to do or of the things you wish to have. Arrange the images in a collage that you can also carry with you on your phone, your laptop or desktop so that you can view it daily. Have your parents or guardians help you in your research by going online, visiting the library, reading books, and learning about the things you want to do or the things you want to have.

The imagination is an incredible tool. It is one of our mental faculties and operates magnificently. The brain knows no difference between what is real and what is imagined. For example, studies show that parts of the brain will light up in an imagined scenario as if the scenario were real.

See Yourself First Person

When delving deep into your imagination, it's important to consider how you visualize yourself. Sometimes, we see ourselves from a bird's-eye view or third person's perspective (look through, look closely at), which is us seeing ourselves through the eyes of another individual. Instead of visualizing yourself from a bird's-eye view or a third-person perspective, try visualizing yourself in the first-person meaning see yourself through YOUR EYES in your imagination.

Imagine yourself being, doing, and having the things you desire. This helps to feed your subconscious mind with the reality you want to create. The subconscious mind, just like the brain, doesn't differentiate between what's real and what's not, so when you see yourself in first person, it's as if you're looking through your own eyes, as you do in the material world. Visualize the world you want to see for yourself. Use your senses to make your imagination even more real (see, smell, taste, sound, and touch). This takes practice, but repetition makes it easier, like learning an instrument or riding a bike.

Your Brain on Imagination

Many people overlook the importance of understanding how their brains and minds function. It is often assumed that imagination is only for children, but in reality, our imagination functions from a structure of our brain called the hippocampus, which is located in the lower hemisphere called the temporal lobe.

Additionally, stress can significantly impact our brain structures, such as the hippocampus and amygdala, the structure of the brain where your emotional responses function. Stress can lead to major issues with using the imagination.

It's important to pay attention to what we are exposed to, as our imagination plays a crucial role in how we see the world around us. The way to heal the brain or repair it is through music. Listening to or playing music lights up many brain parts, including the hippocampus and amygdala. Studies show that music can repair damaged tissues in the brain with its beats, rhythm, and tones, which activate the amygdala - where our emotional responses function - and the right hippocampus - where memory and imagination functions.

Let's be more intentional about what we allow ourselves to read, watch, listen or talk about and take the time to nurture our imagination.

My Imagination Story

Before moving to Watts to live with my aunt and cousins, I lived with my mom and younger brother in a town called Hawthorne. A summer or two before middle school, I discovered a television show called *Bug Juice*. It followed a group of kids at summer camp, and I would watch it imagining I was there, too. The show gave me comfort and helped me feel less alone whenever my younger brother spent time with his father's family.

During my first semester of middle school in Hawthorne, I attended a school with a very well-rounded community. Every year, the new 6th graders went on a three-day camping trip to kick off the middle school experience. I got the chance to go, and while the trip wasn't exactly like *Bug Juice*, it gave me a taste of something I had always wanted—being in a new environment with kids my own age, sharing adventures together.

Looking back, I realize that watching *Bug Juice* so many times planted the experience of summer camp in my mind. Eventually, it became a reality when I went to 6th grade camp.

Mistake to Avoid: Not Using Your Imagination

Not using one of your most powerful mental faculties, the imagination, could possibly rob you of great opportunities you could create for yourself. Imagination is a tool that allows you to mentally construct your future before it happens. It's the bridge between where you are and where you want to be. Without it, you're stuck in the limitations of your current reality, unable to see beyond the obstacles in front of you.

When you choose to not use your imagination, you limit your ability to dream, visualize, and bring forth new possibilities. Instead of thinking beyond your circumstances, you stay confined within them. You miss out on the chance to envision a better future, whether making a new friend, going to a new place or learning a new instrument. Without the practice of using imagination, your mind is less open to new ideas and opportunities that could transform your life.

For me, using my imagination allowed me to create a vivid mental image of attending a camp long before it became a reality. I could see it, feel it, and believe it so strongly that my actions aligned with that vision. If I hadn't tapped into my imagination, I might have settled for less, thinking it was too far out of reach or impossible. But because I envisioned myself there, my belief grew stronger, and I stayed committed to taking the necessary steps.

Imagination works hand-in-hand with desire and vision. It helps you clarify your goals and keeps you motivated when times are tough. Without it, you're left to rely solely on logic and what already exists in your current environment. This can lead to missed opportunities because you're only seeing life as it is, not as it could be.

By not engaging your imagination, you also limit your ability to solve problems creatively. When challenges arise, imagination allows you to think outside the box and come up with innovative solutions. Without it, you may get stuck in frustration, unable to find a way forward. Your dreams remain unfulfilled, not because they're impossible, but because you couldn't see yourself achieving them.

The beauty of imagination is that it gives you permission to explore limitless possibilities. It allows you to dream big, break free from what may be holding you down in your current circumstances (surrounding conditions, situation), and believe in outcomes that haven't yet materialized. Without it, you lose the opportunity to create the opportunities you truly want. You end up accepting less than you deserve because you can't see beyond the immediate challenges.

Don't make the mistake of not using this powerful mental faculty. Imagination is where ideas are born, plans are created, and desires start to come alive. When you actively use it, you open the door to opportunities that otherwise might have gone unnoticed. Imagination not only helps you see what's possible but also gives you the confidence and motivation to pursue it with everything you have.

Next Step

Start by finding a quiet place for at least five minutes to check your visualization or imagery abilities. Can you visualize yourself in the first person? Can you recreate images you have seen or read about? If you aren't able to tap into your imagination, take some time to listen or make music. Music may help jog old memories and even help you produce new ones (listen to some joyful and uplifting lyrics). Practice imagining daily, and soon, imagining yourself as desired will become second nature.

Now that you have done the warm up, complete the exercise and journal prompt below.

Exercise: Guided visualization – imagine a perfect school day where everything goes your way.

Journal Prompt: What did it feel like to imagine that day?

Remember, this is your imagination. Have fun!

4

Power of Thoughts and Words

Our Thoughts Become Things

Our thoughts play a crucial role in achieving our desires. Thoughts are vibrational energy. A Universal Law called the Law of Vibrations states that everything vibrates, nothing rests. Our thoughts are included. We've heard of 'thought waves.' A wave vibrates

Often, our actions and repeated thoughts are closely linked. As we continue to focus on certain thoughts, they gradually seep into our subconscious minds, as discussed in the previous chapter. The subconscious mind is expansive and absorbs everything, ultimately materializing our repeated thoughts into reality. Therefore, it is important to be intentional with our thoughts and their alignment (arrangement in a line) with our desires. Our thoughts are like seeds, and our minds are tied to the soil, nurturing positive and productive thoughts. If our thoughts do not align with our goals, addressing and redirecting them is crucial. We must be intentional in our thoughts, as they have the power to shape our realities. Remember the importance of focusing on positive, constructive thoughts materializing our desires into actions and reality. I'm here to help you shift your mindset and understand the importance of our thoughts in creating the life we truly desire.

My Thought Experience

My middle school in Hawthorne had always been named after the street it was on—for as long as I could remember. A few months into my first semester, the school administrators decided to rename it after someone important. I didn't know who this person was, and I later found out this important person was a Physical Education teacher in the district for many decades.

When I heard about the change, I was completely against it. I didn't like the new name at all. I had been happy with a school named after a street I knew well. The new name felt boring, unfamiliar, and something I couldn't relate to. At least the original name reminded me of places I had traveled often with my mom and younger brother.

I thought about my dislike for the new name so consistently that I somehow found myself at a different middle school the following semester—in a small town called Watts. That middle school was also named after someone I didn't know.

Looking back, I realize that my persistent focus on disliking the name of my first middle school—even though it was in a safe, good neighborhood—may have contributed to my moving to a middle school in a rough environment.

Our Words Create Worlds

In earlier chapters, we discussed the etymology of WORDS and their origins to understand how to use them appropriately when expressing ourselves. Words carry great power; if we are not mindful of our language, we may unintentionally attract or materialize things we do not desire. When you clearly define what the meaning of a word is, you begin to use it in its proper form. People may be more willing to use words properly when they know the word's origin.

Words are deeply linked to our thoughts. As you continue reading, you will realize how carefully chosen words can help materialize your desires or unintentionally bring about what you do not want. Focusing on what you desire and care (to give serious mental attention) to do, be, and have is crucial. When we dwell on what we do not want, those thoughts and words have a way of coming back to us.

Understanding the origin of words, many of which stem from Latin, can help us use them more effectively in creating our desired reality. By learning the true meanings and origins of our words, we can come one step closer to materializing what we truly desire.

My Words Experience

Back to my thoughts about my middle school's name change: I would talk to myself every day about how much I didn't like it. The school was being named after a man I knew nothing about, and I couldn't relate to him at all. At the entrance of the school, there was even a metal sculpture of this person. Every day, I would see it and repeat my dislike for the new name, almost as if I was training my mind to focus on what bothered me.

Not once did I take the time to appreciate or acknowledge the things I actually enjoyed about my middle school—the teachers, the friends, the classes I liked, or the safe, familiar neighborhood. My attention was consumed entirely by what I didn't like.

By the following semester, I found myself attending a different middle school in Watts, named after a medical surgeon I had never heard of. I realize now that my persistent focus on the negative aspects of my first school—the name, the unfamiliar sculpture, and my lack of connection to it—may have influenced my path, leading me to a new environment that would challenge me in ways I hadn't anticipated.

Mistake to Avoid: Misusing Your Thoughts and Words

When we are not intentional with our thoughts and words, we might create worlds for ourselves that we really don't want to live in. Both thoughts and words are incredibly powerful—they act as the architects of our reality. If we misuse them, consciously or unconsciously, we may find ourselves trapped in situations that don't align with our true desires.

Thoughts, the seeds of our internal world, shape the beliefs we hold about ourselves and the world around us. They guide our perceptions, influence our actions, and set the course for what we believe is possible. If our thoughts are filled with doubt, fear, or negativity, those same patterns will reflect in our external experiences. The problem arises when we don't recognize the role our thoughts play in creating our circumstances. Instead of seeing them as the root cause of our struggles, we often place the blame on external situations.

In my own experience, my negative thoughts about the new name of my first middle school led me to a rougher middle school the following semester. The repetitive thoughts I had from my conscious (aware or knowing) mind went to my subconscious (under or below awareness/knowing) mind. This means that my repetitive thoughts about disliking something attracted more dislike in my life. I went from disliking the new name of my first middle school to disliking much of my time at the second middle school.

Similarly, our words are the tools we use to bring those internal thoughts into the external world. Words have creative power—they can either reinforce our desires or perpetuate our doubts. When we speak, we declare our beliefs and intentions to the universe, setting things in motion. If our words reflect self-doubt or worst events, we give life to those beliefs. We affirm our fears and make them more concrete. Over time, this can shape a reality we don't actually want to live in, yet it becomes difficult to escape because we've verbally reinforced it.

For example, I spoke about my dislike of the new name for my first middle school over and over again every day. I had a tougher time by the end of my first year in middle school than when I started.

When we aren't intentional about the words we use, we unintentionally align ourselves with the things we fear rather than the things we desire. Words like "I can't," "I'm not good enough," "That's not for me" or consistently speaking about what or who we "don't like" build walls that limit us from seeing or possessing new opportunities. Our words become self-fulfilling prophecies (to tell beforehand), shaping a world (human existence) of limitations instead of one filled with potential.

The real danger lies in not being aware of this power. When we are careless with our thoughts and words, we unintentionally create a reality that doesn't reflect what we truly want. We end up feeling stuck, frustrated, or defeated, all the while not realizing that we've had the power to change it all along. The more we repeat these terrible thoughts and words, the deeper we become entrenched in a reality that feels out of alignment with our true desires.

To avoid this, we must become intentional. We need to train our minds to think thoughts that align with what we truly want, and we need to speak words that affirm those desires. Just as terrible thoughts and words create barriers, joyful ones can create breakthroughs. By intentionally focusing on thoughts of success, joy, and possibility—and speaking them into existence—we can shape a world that mirrors our highest aspirations.

Next Step

Exercise: "Flip the Script" – write down 3 terrible thoughts and turn them into joyful or successful ones.

Journal Prompt: What's the most victorious (the word 'vict-' means "to conquer" or "to win") thing I can say to myself every morning?

5

Subconscious Mind and the "How"

In previous chapters I briefly discuss the subconscious mind. Let's go deeper in this one. In this chapter I explain the importance of the subconscious mind in attracting our true desires.

Let's break down the word subconscious. The word "sub" means 'under or below' and the word "conscious" means 'aware or know'. When we bring the two back together, we get the meaning 'under awareness' or 'below knowing'. So that we have a clearer understanding of how our conscious and subconscious minds operate, imagine we are at a beach and looking out into the ocean. On the surface we see a ship, some birds snatching up fish, and might see a dolphin or whale appear. All these things on the surface are our conscious mind. Under the water, is the bottom of the ship along with creatures under water. Everything under the water is the subconscious mind.

Our conscious mind is the 'thinking' mind. Our subconscious mind is where the thoughts turn into action without us knowing most of the time. The subconscious is usually on "autopilot".

The foundation of materialization lies in our subconscious mind, one of several minds that function differently within us. As we go about our daily lives, our conscious (aware or knowing) mind forms our thoughts, while our subconscious mind, present from birth, operates continuously. Our subconscious mind takes shape between the ages of zero to five or six, shaping our thoughts, intellect, reasoning, and willpower based on the influences of our environment, guardians, relatives, and experiences. The subconscious mind has the ability to remember everything and shape your reality.

Subconscious Mind is the HOW

Our subconscious mind internalizes every detail, regardless of whether it is joyful or terrible. Our spoken and unspoken thoughts eventually become the essence of our subconscious mind, attracting vibrations that align with our internalized beliefs. The body reflects these vibrations, attracting experiences and occurrences that resonate with our subconscious programming. Thus, our forgotten or even fleeting thoughts and words fall deep within our subconscious, shaping our life experiences. All that the subconscious mind takes in and is impressed upon is the HOW that makes everything for your desire to come to reality.

One challenge we face is the conflicting messages we allow ourselves to absorb (to drink in, to swallow). Have you ever wondered why something you long for seems out of reach? I have experienced this myself. Upon discovering the power of the subconscious mind and its ability to absorb and process our thoughts and experiences, I realized that I was attracting things that resonated with past experiences and repetitive thoughts, such as attending a school that had a name I could relate to.

In the last chapter, I talked about how much I didn't like the name my first middle school was being changed to and how my dislike for it led me to my second middle school in the same school year. Now, what I didn't mention was why I felt strongly disconnected to the name of the first middle school and who my second middle school was named after. I later in life realized that my dislike for the name of my middle school in Hawthorne was much deeper than I had expected.

My Subconscious Mind Experience

In the previous chapter, I shared my story about not liking the new name my first middle school was adopting because I couldn't relate to it. The following semester, I ended up attending a middle school in a rough area.

Looking back, I realize my reaction was shaped by my elementary school experience. I attended a private Christian elementary school where almost everyone—students, teachers, the principal, even cafeteria staff—looked like me. Our performances celebrated pride, power, and freedom for people who shared my skin tone. Almost every year, we performed for Black History Month and Christmas, singing and acting to music by artists who reflected me. That environment impressed on my subconscious what was familiar, relatable, and inspiring.

When my first middle school changed its name to honor someone who didn't look like me, it felt foreign and unrelatable. My subconscious had been trained to connect with places where I saw myself reflected, and this change clashed with that internal template.

The following semester, I moved to a school named after a man who had a copper-skinned complexion like mine and was a pioneering medical surgeon. I didn't realize it at the time, but my subconscious immediately resonated with this connection. Seeing someone like me in the very identity of the school gave me a sense of belonging even with the school being in a rough area— before I consciously understood why.

Looking back, I can see how my elementary school conditioning shaped my thoughts, feelings, and choices. It guided me toward environments where representation mattered, showing me the subtle but powerful role the subconscious plays in what we relate to, notice, and ultimately pursue.

Mistake to Avoid: Not Filtering Input

The subconscious mind does NOT know the difference between our REAL experiences and our IMAGINED experiences. It is constantly taking in information, processing thoughts, emotions, and external stimuli, whether we are aware of it or not. It acts as the engine behind the scenes, working tirelessly to materialize the reality we live in based on the information we allow into it. If we are not careful about what we feed our subconscious—whether through thoughts, words, what we watch, or the people we surround ourselves with—it will materialize outcomes based on this unfiltered input. The "how" of our lives, the way situations unfold, is directly influenced by the contents of our subconscious mind.

When we don't give proper attention to intentionally direct our subconscious, it starts to work with whatever input it receives. It doesn't filter out fearful thoughts or unwanted suggestions on its own—it simply takes in everything and shapes our reality accordingly. If we allow doubts, fears, limiting beliefs, or the worst of others to fill our minds, we give those things the power to control the "how" of our lives. This often leads to undesired outcomes, situations that feel out of our control, and situations that leave us feeling trapped or stuck.

For example, if we constantly think, "I don't know how I'll ever afford this" or "I'm not smart enough," the subconscious mind accepts these thoughts as truths. It then begins to create experiences that align with these beliefs. Instead of opening doors or finding unexpected opportunities, it closes them, reinforcing the horrible perceptions we've allowed in. You may find yourself missing out on chances simply because your subconscious was programmed to believe they weren't possible.

When you shift your focus to your desires and trust your subconscious mind, it starts to work on the 'how' for you. Just like when I thought and expressed my dislike for my first middle school's name change led to me attending a middle school named after someone who looked like me. My subconscious mind had been programmed in elementary school through performances and singing songs that were about the pride, power and freedom of my people.

The key takeaway is this: *if we don't purposefully direct our subconscious mind, we risk letting the "how" of life take shape based on random, unfiltered input.* This often results in unwanted situations that seem beyond our control. The subconscious mind is neutral; it simply brings into reality whatever it is fed. That's why it's essential to be mindful of the thoughts, ideas, and beliefs we consistently entertain, as they influence the "how" in ways we may not realize.

By filling your subconscious with empowering, winning thoughts and focusing on your desired outcomes, you train it to find solutions, open doors, and align situations in your favor. But if you leave it to chance, feeding it a mix of uncertainty, fear, and doubt, the "how" will reflect those things, often leading to results that do not serve you.

In short, be intentional with what you allow your subconscious mind to absorb. Your thoughts, words, and beliefs are the seeds, and the subconscious is the soil. Whether those seeds grow into the life you desire or into a garden full of weeds depends entirely on the quality of what you plant.

Your Next Step

The subconscious mind is often overlooked but holds the key to unlocking our true desires. In this age of information, we have the opportunity to explore and understand the power of the subconscious mind. It is crucial to take the time to reflect on the repetitive thoughts that have not benefited us and address the root causes of our challenges. We can align our thoughts and actions with what we genuinely desire by rewriting our fearful experiences and consistently focusing on our true desires through affirmations and visualization.

This deliberate practice will allow our bodies to resonate at the frequency of our true desires.

Exercise: Create a "Daily Affirmation Card."

Journal Prompt: What phrase would I like to repeat to myself every day?

6

CopyCat

This chapter delves into the importance of seeking out individuals who have achieved what you desire. It's not just about finding anyone who has achieved what you aspire to, but rather finding someone with whom you truly connect and who is doing that thing you want the best. Take the time to research this person and learn about their background, upbringing, and what led them to where they are today. Dive into interviews, books, and any other available resources to truly understand their journey. If this person offers classes or books, I encourage you to take advantage of these opportunities. And if you know someone personally who has done what you desire to do, follow that person's blueprint if you know them to be credible (worthy to be believed). Take the time to understand who has mentored them and learn from their mentor as well. Consider visiting the places that have been influential in their journey, such as their school or any institutions that have played a role in their success.

Take Notes

By immersing yourself in their world, you have the opportunity to learn from their experiences and gain valuable knowledge in a much shorter period of time. Embracing this approach could significantly accelerate your own path to success, potentially reducing the time it takes to achieve your goals from decades to just a few years or even less.

Studying the journeys of others is a crucial step in achieving your desires and establishing your vision.

My Copycat Experience

While attending middle school in Watts, I looked up to my favorite music artist, Lauryn Hill. I admired her character in the film *Sister Act 2: Back in the Habit* so much that I would dress like her character at school. I had watched *Sister Act 2* countless times during elementary school—teachers often played it nearly every Friday after school. By the time I reached middle school, I had probably seen the film over 100 times.

I listened to Lauryn Hill's album *The Miseducation of Lauryn Hill* over and over again, memorizing some of her iconic rap verses. I talked about her constantly to my 6th-grade instructor. One day, my teacher even brought a well-known magazine called *Essence* to class and had me sit next to her to read an article about Lauryn Hill during an entire class period. She also allowed us to watch Lauryn Hill's *MTV Unplugged* on VHS for one of our classes.

I would perform Lauryn Hill's rhymes as if they were my own during P.E. Later, I began writing poetry consistently, inspired by her lyrics. Lauryn Hill was one of the two main reasons I wanted to learn how to play guitar.

Even as an adult, I've continued to study her artistry. I wanted to know how to sing like Lauryn Hill in *Sister Act 2*, and I've danced to the song "His Eye Is on the Sparrow" from the movie's soundtrack in church.

I've studied Ms. Lauryn Hill for decades, and her influence has shaped not only my music but my creativity, my performance, and my love for artistic expression.

Being a "copycat" of Lauryn Hill taught me something important: imitation can be a powerful tool for growth. By studying her lyrics, performances, and style, I absorbed techniques, rhythms, and expressions that became the foundation of my own artistic voice. What started as copying turned into creating—taking inspiration from someone I admired and using it to develop my own creativity, performance skills, and love for artistic expression.

Mistake to Avoid: Not Asking for Help

In your journey, you may have encountered times when not speaking up about your desires or not seeking out guidance from others has slowed down your progress or caused unnecessary struggles. When I look back on my experience, had I not talked to my 6th instructor about playing the guitar, had she not told me to "ask your parents, the worst they could say is 'no,'" I would have missed out on a great opportunity to play music. Both my teacher and my family helped me to get closer to copying Lauryn Hill in middle school because I asked for their help.

If we don't actively speak up about our interests to those who can help us like our parents or guardians, teachers, or someone we know who is doing or having what we want, we risk missing out on guidance that can help us reach our desires faster. It's easy to think we have to figure it all out on our own, but that often leads to unnecessary hurdles or wasted time.

When we don't ask for help or don't observe others who have already achieved what we want, we create longer, more difficult paths for ourselves. Whether it's because of pride, fear of rejection, or simply not realizing how valuable their experience can be, the result is often the same: frustration, delays, and missed opportunities.

By learning from others and copying their methods, you can avoid more mistakes and instead, move closer to your desires with much greater ease. Just like I trusted my teacher's advice and did what she advised, you can do the same with your goals.

There's no shame in copying a proven path—in fact, it's one of the smartest ways to ensure you're on track to your desires.

Next Step

When setting your desires, seek credible individuals who achieve what you aspire to and follow the blueprint of the one you resonate with the most.

Exercise: Imagine being in your role model's shoes—what's one choice they would make differently than you?

Journal Prompt: What's one quality I admire in them that I want to grow in myself?

PART 3 - HAVE

Express gratitude and appreciation and understand your W.H.Y. To 'HAVE' means "to own, possess, be subject to, and experience."

7

W.H.Y.

Your W.H.Y.

Understanding the reason behind your desire is important in reaching your goal. Your WHY is critical - it drives you to take the necessary steps. An acronym for "why" is "what hurts you." Often, our past pains are the driving force behind our goals. This ties back to an earlier chapter in the book where we discussed finding solutions to problems, sometimes stemming from hurtful past experiences. Your "why" can start the change you want to see in your life, propelling you toward your goal. Once you uncover your why, the other steps to reaching your goal will become clear. Finding your purpose is critical.

Define Your Purpose

In defining your purpose, one of the most powerful places to start is by understanding what deeply affects you—what hurts you. Often, the source of your purpose lies within your pain, struggles, or frustrations, either from your own experiences or those you've witnessed around you. Perhaps it's a challenge you've personally faced, a problem you've observed in your community, or a troubling situation from your past that continues to weigh on your heart. By reflecting on what stirs you emotionally, you can identify what truly matters to you. This awareness is crucial because it gives your vision depth and authenticity.

The most common mistake people make when pursuing their vision is not having a strong enough "why." Without a compelling reason that pulls you forward, it's easy to lose motivation when obstacles arise. But when your "why" is rooted in something that truly moves you, especially when it's connected to helping others, it becomes more than just a goal—it becomes a mission. A purpose centered around making a difference for others has the power to sustain you, even during the most difficult times.

When your vision extends beyond personal gain and aligns with the idea of serving a greater good, your passion naturally grows stronger. Your "why" becomes a source of inspiration not only for yourself but also for those around you. A purpose-driven life gives your vision the fuel it needs to become a reality.

Your desire and vision, when tied to a higher purpose, become forces of change, motivating you to persevere regardless of the challenges you face.

My W.H.Y. Experience

One vision (or visions) I had back in 6th or 7th grade that I've held onto all the way into adulthood was to be a stay-at-home mother, run my own businesses from home to contribute to my household, and use those businesses to purchase land for my family. Today, I am a stay-at-home mother and wife, actively creating ways to earn money from my creativity. Soon, I will purchase land for my family to live on.

I had a burning desire to achieve this vision (or visions). What was my WHY? I had a few reasons.

Growing up with only my mother's side of the family, I spent summers mostly by myself. My brother and my cousins were with their father's family. I had no connection to my father's side. My father had three other daughters—my younger sisters—but I never saw them after my 7th grade year. Having experienced that sense of absence shortly after entering middle school, I was eager to have a big family of my own.

My mother became a single parent to me and my younger brother shortly after I entered middle school. She worked long hours, getting up at 3 a.m., leaving home by 5 a.m., and not returning until 6 p.m. Weekends for her were often spent doing chores, spending some time with me and my brother, and connecting with other adults. Watching her work the way she did and noticing how little time we had together, I knew that when I became a parent, I wanted to stay home with my sons and daughters. I was determined to be their educator, parent, guidance counselor, and primary caretaker.

Seeing how much my mother worked away from home also inspired me to figure out a way to earn money from home.

Living in Watts during my middle school years was tough. We lived where we could afford, and I saw firsthand the challenges of renting property owned by someone else. The property we lived on was owned by my grandmother's former neighbor, and my relatives paid him rent. I knew this property owner personally, and he became another reason I wanted to own my own land and rental properties— so my family could live wherever we chose.

My WHY for these visions—being a stay-at-home parent, earning income from home, and owning land—helped me hold onto them for more than 20 years. These early experiences shaped my intentions and strengthened my determination to create the life I imagined for myself and my family.

Mistake to Avoid: Not Having a Compelling WHY

When you don't have a compelling WHY—when you haven't clearly identified "What Hurts You"— you run the risk of losing momentum or even feeling ready in your pursuit of a desire or vision. Without that deep-rooted purpose driving you forward, the challenges you face can seem like a lot to handle, and your goals might start to feel out of reach. Have you ever felt like giving up because things became too hard or the obstacles seemed too great? If so, it's possible that your purpose—your "why"—wasn't fully defined.

I experienced this while trying to get into my middle school band. My "WHY" was not strong enough for me to push past that magnet counselor's "No" to me getting into the magnet to get in the band. I didn't attempt any other time. I didn't ask more questions because I didn't have a "WHY" to push me to get a "YES!"

If you don't take the time to figure out your "why," you may end up pursuing a goal that doesn't align with your true passions or one that lacks the emotional weight needed to keep you going. This disconnect can lead to frustration, burnout, or even giving up altogether. But when you identify the core reason behind your desire—especially if it's rooted in something that has caused you pain or something you deeply care about—you'll find the strength and resilience to keep moving forward, even when the journey becomes difficult. My twenty-plus year vision(s) I held on to is because of what hurt me. The journey to get where I am today was tough with many obstacles in my way. I let none of those obstacles stop me from being a stay-at-home mother and wife and now creating ways to contribute to my household monetarily.

So, take the time to reflect on your own "What Hurts You." Is there something that stirs you to act? Maybe it's a personal challenge you've faced or an injustice you've seen on the planet that you want to change. Whatever it is, make sure your purpose is connected to something that matters deeply to you. When your purpose is clear, it doesn't just give you a reason to chase your vision; it gives you the motivation and grit to overcome any obstacle that stands in your way. Your purpose becomes the fire that keeps your desire alive, no matter how hard the road gets.

Next Step

Exercise: Write your own "Why Statement" about one vision you have.

Journal Prompt: Why does this vision matter to me, and how will it make my life better?

8

Gratitude and Appreciation

Since many of us use Gratitude and appreciation interchangeably, I will be expressing how both are fundamental pillars of materializing. It requires being thankful and estimating the quality and worth of something for what we already have and believing we will receive what we desire. Expressing gratitude/appreciation has a powerful effect on our bodies; it neutralizes hopelessness and elevates our vibrations. Having a grateful/appreciative mindset deflects anything that does not align with our desires. It opens us up to new possibilities and higher vibrations. By acknowledging what we're grateful for and appreciating what we already have, we can see that with the right mindset, we can achieve our true desires.

Difference between Gratitude and Appreciation

The etymology of 'Gratitude' meaning "goodwill," from Latin *gratus,* means "thankfulness, pleasing." PIE root 'gwere' meaning "to favor".

The etymology of 'Appreciation' means "act of estimating the quality and worth of something," from Late Latin *appretiare* meaning "estimate the quality of". 'Appreciate', "to estimate or value highly" from Late Latin *appretiare* {break the word down} from *ad* which means "to" + *pretium* which means "price".

Your Brain on Gratitude

Expressing gratitude daily can rewire the brain through the process of neuroplasticity, which is the brain's ability to form and reorganize synaptic connections, especially in response to learning or experience. When you consistently practice gratitude, your brain begins to create new neural pathways that are specifically associated with feelings of appreciation and joyfulness. Each time you focus on gratitude, those pathways are activated and reinforced, making it easier and more natural for you to access feelings of thankfulness in the future.

Over time, this practice leads to a shift in the brain's default mode—where it naturally starts to focus more on the positive aspects of life rather than dwelling on hopelessness. As a result, not only does your mindset become more joyful, but you also start to experience greater emotional resilience, improved mental well-being, and an overall sense of happiness. Your brain essentially "adapts" to this new pattern of thinking, making gratitude a powerful tool for fostering long-term happiness and emotional health.

My Experience with Gratitude and Appreciation

Gratitude and appreciation are simple acknowledgments of the good that's happened or is happening in your life.

When my aunt and cousins moved to Watts, they lived in the front house on my granny's neighbor's rental property. Later that same year, I moved into my aunt's house while my mother, granny, and brother moved into one of the four apartments in the back on the same property.

Shortly after moving in with my aunt and cousins, my aunt created a system for me and my twin cousin to clean the kitchen. We had been doing this system for about a year when I decided to ask my aunt for an allowance. She responded, "Your allowance is me allowing you to stay in my house!"

Her response completely shifted the way I looked at life. I began to see the value in both the big and small things around me. I learned to be grateful for what I already had before asking for anything else. I took better care of my belongings, showing appreciation for them.

One memory that sticks with me is when I stayed at a friend's house as a teenager. I noticed the little things—how tidy their rooms were, how the family prepared meals, even the chores they performed. I helped wherever I could, cleaned up after myself, and treated their home with care. I did this not because anyone told me to, but because I was grateful for being welcomed and treated generously.

This early lesson taught me that gratitude isn't just a feeling—it's a practice. Recognizing and appreciating the blessings you already have created a mindset that draws even more joyfulness into your life. The more I practiced gratitude, the more I noticed joy in everyday moments, from a meal shared with family to having a safe place to sleep. Gratitude became the foundation for how I approached life and relationships.

Mistake to Avoid: Lacking Gratitude and Appreciation

If we don't practice gratitude and appreciation, it's easy to lose sight of the blessings already present in our lives. A lack of gratitude and appreciation creates a mindset where we are always chasing after what we don't have, feeling as though something is missing. In doing so, we not only overlook the resources, relationships, and opportunities right in front of us, but we also rob ourselves of the joy that comes with acknowledging what's good in our current situation.

In my experience, asking for an allowance from my aunt may be a light situation. My aunt's response really helped me to acknowledge that she was allowing me to live in her home and she was giving me freedoms that I was not getting while living with my mother.

The moment I shifted the way I looked at my living situation at my aunt's house and began to express genuine gratitude for the roof over my head and the freedom I had, everything started to change. I realized that cleaning the kitchen was a minor gesture of appreciation and gratitude I had to display.

For many people, the mistake is thinking that we will be grateful only once we achieve our goals or get what we desire. But in reality, practicing gratitude right now can create the space for more opportunities, support, and fulfilling experiences to come into our lives. When we don't show appreciation for what we already have, it's easy to fall into a mindset of lack, always searching for something outside of ourselves to fill the void.

By neglecting gratitude, we risk living in a state of dissatisfaction, unable to appreciate what's already working in our favor. This can make the journey to achieving our desires feel longer and more challenging, because we aren't fully grounded in the present moment. When we express gratitude, we remind ourselves of our blessings, stay connected to what's important, and invite more abundance into our lives. Gratitude can turn what we already have into enough and we can attract even more of what we desire.

Next Step

My suggestion to the reader is to hold back complaining too much about what you lack and focus on expressing gratitude/appreciation for what you do have, no matter how small. This simple shift in mindset can reveal the abundance already present and align us with the people and opportunities that can help us achieve our desires. Stop complaining and speak genuinely about the things and people for whom you are grateful/appreciative. Doing so allows you to open yourselves up to the solutions and support you need to bring your vision to life.

Exercise: Create a "Gratitude Jar" (real or on paper).

Journal Prompt: What's one small thing I'm grateful for today?

To the Reader

(Summary)

This book is a roadmap to help you achieve the results you seek. Embrace your vision every day. Your imagination is a powerful tool, so don't be afraid to use it! Remember that everything you use in your daily life, from your bed to the space shuttle, originated from someone's imagination. Be intentional in your thoughts, words, and actions, and practice, drill, and rehearse the life you want to create. Focus on yourself first before trying to help others. Once you become adept (completely skilled) at achieving your goals, your success will be evident to others, and they will be curious about your methods. Then, you can share your wisdom with confidence. Remember, you are in control.

MY APPRECIATION

Much appreciation to every student, every parent, every educator, every school, every district for picking up this book and applying the content and sharing your results.

About the Author

Alexandria Patterson was born and raised in South Central Los Angeles to a Californian mother and a Costa Rican father. She was primarily raised by her mother's family and her younger brother's father's family, with limited contact with her father from ages 7 to 12. As a result, Alexandria had little knowledge of her Costa Rican heritage.

Growing up, Alexandria turned to various art forms to fill the void left by her father's absence, using her imagination to create the environments she longed for. During her junior year in high school, she discovered an interest in filmmaking. In her senior year, she received three Video in the Classroom Awards for the Los Angeles Unified School District for her high school Public Service Announcement short film televised on KLCS (an instructional television station for LAUSD) in Los Angeles.

Alexandria moved to Nevada with her partner after studying at The Los Angeles Film School and the University of California, Los Angeles.

Nevada is where she reconnected with her father and paternal family for the first time in almost two decades.

Alexandria graduated from The Los Angeles Film School with her Associate Degree in Film/Cinema and a Bachelor's Degree in African-

American Studies from the University of California, Los Angeles.

She now lives with her partner and their son, continuing to imagine their best lives and enjoy gratifying experiences together.